Help!

I'M ADOPTING A CHILD

Personal Insights from an Adoptive Parent

PATRICA DOPEMU

ISBN Paperback: 978-1-8383971-0-4

ISBN eBook: 978-1-8383971-1-1

Cover and inner design by Andy at meadencreative.com

CONTENTS

ACKNOWLEDGEMENTS

I give all glory and thanks to God Almighty for giving me the wisdom, knowledge, inspiration and strength to write this book.

To my husband, for his tremendous support and contribution in all aspects of the development and structure of the manuscript. Thank you for always being there for me in all I do. You rock!

To our daughter and her family, thank you for your continuous support in many ways, you have been a 'big sister' indeed.

To our older son for reading through and correcting some of the grammar, I know you are more English than I am—thank you! And to our youngest son, without whom this book would not exist. He has been so excited about it from the beginning. Thank you for going into your archives and bringing out all those old pictures and paintings. I love you both and thank God for your lives daily.

Last but surely not the least, Naomi, my dear friend of many years, for taking the time to read the manuscript and for your kind and touching words, thank you.

FOREWORD

Giving, touching others' lives, expanding the circle of our concern to include others, being totally selfless and being always open to receive unconditionally, perfectly describes the author of this wonderful book.

I met Patricia at University nearly 25 years ago, both mature students striving to become the best we can. Life eventually took us both on very different journeys, I went on to qualify as a family lawyer whilst Patricia, amongst other things, went on to do one of the kindest acts in humanity - providing a vulnerable child with a permanent, loving and secure home.

It is not for all and there cannot be any criticism, but for those who are considering this act of kindness, the book not only provides the Law in relation to adoption, but also a raw and personal journey of the adoption process itself. It goes into detail of not only the wonderful highs, but also the lows that Patricia and indeed all her family had encountered. She has done this with such dazzling skill that I soon realised how profoundly it touched my heart.

Naomi Yeshua.
Family Law Solicitor.

PREFACE

There is a massive reluctance, especially in my community, to adopt children. I must admit that in the initial stages of our own adoption process, I had a lot of unanswered questions in my head; this made me a bit uncertain about how everything would work. Even though I had the desire to adopt a child for so many years, I was sceptical about the whole process. I read, researched and spoke with a few families who had adopted children, but I did not find examples to draw from amongst people who had similar backgrounds to mine. A number of people did not think it was a good idea to adopt, as they viewed adoption as raising someone else's child, a child they believed would eventually leave or even go back to their biological family, leaving the adoptive family with regret and hurt after all they had been through.

Living with members of extended family or even unrelated persons is not really alien in African communities, where it is traditional to live together as family and to look out for one another. Within these cultures, when families take care of other people's children, there are no legal obligations or expressed rules, regulations or government policies imposed. Children living within any family setting are simply obliged to contribute to the home by way of helping out with the household chores and other things needed for the smooth running of the home (just as the biological children do), whilst the parents or guardian are obliged to provide a home, food, clothing, educate and raise the child accordingly. It is a family, a partnership.

The system in the Western world is totally different, and it is viewed by some as too lengthy. The intrusive nature of the adoption process in the UK and the obligations imposed on adoptive parents are what some find difficult. For these reasons not many prospective African parents come forward for adoption.

My husband and I sat down, and together we analysed the various views and comments. We came to the conclusion that a child does not belong completely to anyone; ultimately, adults are only custodians. In addition, we could see how rules, policies and regulations bring accountability, ensuring the safety and well-being of the child. The process also gives the adoptive family guidelines. Overall, it guarantees protection for both adoptive families and adopted children. Having gone through the whole adoption process, and then bringing our son home and seeing him grow every day has been one of the most rewarding things I could ever experience.

When we adopted, it further highlighted the fact that even our own biological children would eventually leave home in pursuit of their own lives, but it is the love, care and upbringing we have given them that matters the most. That bond is the string that attaches us forever: the good and not-so-good times we shared, times of joy and laughter, moments of correction and rebuke, times we were there for them through thick and thin, plus all the 'family times.' Those experiences are the most significant in the long run.

We had the space in our home, lots of love in our hearts and lots of parenting experience from raising our biological children and we were not going to allow these valuable assets to go to waste. We therefore decided that we were going to adopt a child, raising them like our own, with that life-long connection of being part of a family. It all worked out as planned, and we are glad it did.

For us, the advantages of raising another child in our home continue to outweigh any inconvenience or challenge involved, and the reward is priceless! It wasn't all without some tough times and challenges along the way, but together we worked through them. That is what family is all about.

Patricia Dopemu

United Kingdom
December 2020

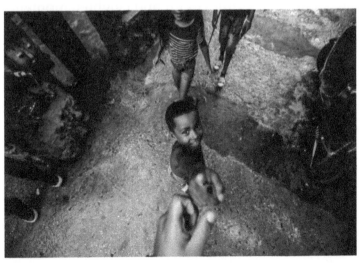

> Belonging to a family is a natural and vital component of life, and every child deserves to be a member of a loving and nurturing family.

Ronald Reagan

INTRODUCTION

One adopts and raises a child, who might otherwise struggle to find their way, in a world that can be lonely, cruel and confusing, providing a loving home, a sense of belonging, and a focus and direction in life. The purpose of this book is to encourage more people to choose adoption; it is a gift that money cannot buy. It would also be useful for those who have already adopted children and are looking to learn from other people's experiences.

This book does not cover the adoption process in detail, but rather gives a few tips to help anyone considering adoption, presenting our own experience of adopting our son, what we have learned in that course and how we have dealt with various issues and challenges. Reflections are also offered about how we have successfully integrated and bonded as a family.

WHY DO PEOPLE ADOPT?

The decision to adopt a child is very personal to the prospective adoptive parents, and there are a variety of reasons why different families would decide to adopt. Some people choose to care for children of family members or other relatives who cannot care for them for any number of reasons, perhaps even due to bereavement. Adoption could then mean keeping the children within the same family circle, with all the legal rights they might have with their biological parents.

I have also met couples who adopted due to medical concerns. Infertility might mean a couple is unable to have children of their own, and therefore opt for adoption as an alternative. Other couples have inheritable genetic diseases and may decide to adopt children rather than possibly transmit those disorders. Some single people are ready to start a family and others adopt children because they have a desire to be a blessing and contribute to society. Considering that there are so many children in care, they just want to give these children a positive experience of belonging to and being part of a family. In fact, some people adopt children over and over again, just because they adore children and love having a large family.

In addition, as a Christian, I believe that adoption as heirs to the promise of salvation is very dear to God's heart. The Bible says that we have been adopted into the family of God's Kingdom: "God decided in advance to adopt us into His own family by bringing us to Himself through Jesus Christ..." (Ephesians 1:5, NLT). One of the key prophets in the Bible, Moses, who would have been killed otherwise, was instead raised by an adoptive mother, becoming instrumental in securing freedom from Pharaoh, the King of Egypt, for the enslaved children of Israel.

Overall, many people adopt because they believe all children deserve to be part of a loving family and to enjoy the amazing experience that the adoption journey brings. In any case, a decision to adopt doesn't only enable these people to form a family; it also gives the *children* the opportunity to belong and be part of that family. Adoption provides loving and stable homes and families for children who need them, and that truly is a beautiful thing.

"You don't have to give birth to have a family. We're all family – an extended family.

Sandra Bullock

THE ADOPTION PROCESS

The adoption of a child is generally defined as 'the act or process of establishing a legal relationship between a child and a parent other than the child's biological parent, thereby entrusting the designated adult with responsibility for raising the child.' The adoptive parents legally assume total parental responsibility for a child, permanently.

This book refers to the adoption process in the United Kingdom (UK) and to our own experiences as adoptive parents. In the UK, a child must be under the age of 18, while the adoptive parents must be 21 years of age or older at the time the adoption application is made. There is no upper age limit for adoptive parents, but they are expected to have the health and energy required to raise a child.

A child can only be adopted if they have been taken into care by a local authority. Children in care are those being 'looked after' by a local authority, including children subject to care orders under

Section 31 of the Children Act 1989 (children cared for by government agencies based on "ill-treatment or the impairment of health or development") and children looked after on a voluntary basis through an agreement with their parents or the intervention of Children's Services. These also include children who are being fostered, living at home with their parents under the supervision of social services or placed by the local authority in various residential or children's homes.

Despite the minimal requirements for adoptive parents, there were 72,590 children in care in the UK as of 31 March 2017, and only 3% of these children would be adopted within a year. A large number of them would end up being raised by foster families. In some cases, the children might live in several families or foster homes before their eighteenth birthdays, this leaves so many children uncertain about their futures. In contrast, a child in care can be adopted by a 'Forever Family' as their own biological child, with the child no longer having legal ties with their biological parents and their name changed to that of their adoptive family.

However, the current legal adoption process is quite lengthy and cumbersome. In the last few years there have been attempts by the UK government to speed up the adoption process, but the figures from the Office of National Statistics (2015 through 2016) on the looked-after children in England showed that these changes have not been achieving the desired results. In fact, there has been a 12% drop in the number of children adopted during that period. As a result, as of 31 March 2018, the number of children looked after by local authorities in England increased, up 4% to 75,420 from 72,590 in 2017.

Despite suggestions and attempts to reduce the time frame and revisions to speed up the adoption process, it will likely still end up being lengthy. Why? *Because numerous thorough, in-depth checks need to be carried out to ensure the safety of each adopted child.* The aim is always to serve the child's best interests, particularly since such children may have been removed from parental custody or placed in care because their homes had been deemed unsafe for their well-being. Therefore, it becomes doubly important that everything be checked out carefully prior to an adoption placement.

"My life has been shaped by the decision two people made over 24 years ago. They decided to adopt a child. They got me, and I got a chance at the kind of life all children deserve.

Karen Fowler

HOW OUR ADOPTION JOURNEY BEGAN

My husband and I initially contacted three different local authorities for adoption, but we did not receive any response from two of them. The third one got back to us. Once they made contact, we hit the ground running, right up until the time we finally brought our son home. The whole adoption process took about two years for us. The time frame would depend on many different factors and personal circumstances. Also, while there are some private agencies you can work with, we decided to apply through a local authority.

In our case we had talked about adopting a child for as long as we had known each other, even before we got married. Our plan was to have our own children first, then at the right time, we would bring other children to become part of our family. The way we envisaged things was that we must be very comfortable financially (or even rich!) before exploring adoption. However, it all happened at a time we least expected, beginning with a casual chat with one of my clients at the time, who put me in touch with someone at the borough's Children's Services Department.

When we decided to adopt, we already had our own biological children and a grandchild. But we believed that we had so much more to give emotionally and physically. We wanted to give back to society by bringing a child into our family and giving that child an opportunity to be loved and cared for, a chance for a bright future and a better experience growing up in a warm and caring home. We found the process long, time-consuming and emotionally challenging. However, as we were quite determined from the outset, we did not allow any of the challenges to discourage us.

The Initial Presentation

Our adoption process started off with a two-hour presentation by a group of social workers from the local authority. These presentations can be quite detailed, but adoptive parents are not expected to remember everything. There were also other prospective adoptive parents present, and we all asked clarifying questions and got other general information. The meeting gave us a good, general overview of the process, and we were able to ask more specific questions later on a one-to-one basis. We then got booked for the next stage: the home visit

The Home Visit

The next step, the home visit, is almost like getting your house ready for the arrival of a new baby. You need to prepare a room, or, in some cases, multiple rooms, depending on the number of children you plan to adopt. Even if it's not fully decorated, the social workers would come to see the home before the process begins, just to ensure that it's suitable and to get a better feel for the family environment.

Prior to the visit, they booked a date with us, and two social workers arrived at our home for inspection. They examined the room we had prepared and looked through our house and garden. They also did a general inspection of our surroundings. We have a big fish pond in our garden, for example, which they advised would need to be professionally secured with a sturdy frame as a safety precaution. It didn't matter that we had raised our own biological child in the same environment; the social workers had to address any risks. We were also advised to cover all the electrical sockets around our home and advised about other general health and safety issues that they observed.

Our fish pond is lovely, but it had to be secured.

They also wanted to know why we had decided to adopt, and they highlighted some of the possible challenges of adoption. They enquired about our preferences with regards to the age range and gender, and asked if we would consider sibling groups, twins or triplets. The number of children you could adopt may also depend on the amount of space or spare rooms available in your home, among other issues. So, we decided on only one child, in part because we only had a single available bedroom.

We had to wait to learn whether our home was deemed suitable, and if so, what the next step would be. To our delight, we got the call a few days later informing us that our spare room was appropriate for housing a child! The next stage was the mandatory preparation course. Again, dates were fixed, we arranged time off from work and eagerly looked forward to taking the course.

Mandatory Four-Day Preparation Course

Our preparation course spanned four full days over a long weekend, and it took us on an emotional roller coaster. The aim was for us to learn more about the adoption process. The course went through various child-related issues, case studies and videos, with examples of real-life children and families. Some of the scenarios and circumstances we saw were heart-breaking.

Adoptive families were invited to the course to share their experiences, as well as some adults who had been adopted as children, in order to give us the adopted child's perspective. They gave insights into how they felt and coped, as well as what changes they would like to see with regards to the whole process and how they have moved on in life.

The course was a massive eye-opener for us, answering a lot of the questions on our minds and putting many of our anxieties to rest. We left feeling more determined to go ahead with the process, regardless of whatever obstacles we might encounter. As part of the course, we were given a piece of homework, entitled "What We Bring to Adoption as We Are Now." As we wrote the bullet points about what we had and could offer as prospective adoptive parents, we felt more positive and convinced that not only were we ready to start the journey, but that it was the right thing to do.

Four other couples and a single parent participated in our course, and because we were together for four full days, we became well acquainted. We exchanged contact details and kept in touch, encouraging and supporting each other and exchanging ideas and information. The group worked really well, and we strengthened each other. Each family within the group eventually followed through with the process, and we all adopted children, including one couple who actually adopted twin brothers.

Some aspects of the course could be overwhelming, and it may even get you wondering whether you want to carry on or even if you made the right decision. Therefore, it's advisable to read various case studies and learn as much about the subject as possible beforehand. You may also want to speak with various agencies. If so, be prepared to ask as many questions as possible. A plethora of information is also accessible on the Adoption UK website and through many other government agencies as well. Also, you'll need to process a large amount of information over the four-day period, which requires concentration and can be draining. Therefore, if possible, dedicate that time solely to taking the course.

What we will bring to adoption as we are now

- We will bring our time, commitment and dedication to walk through the process of being adoptive parents

- We will come with open minds to learn and share with others for a clearer understanding of the issues relating to adoption.

- We are coming with hearts full of love and compassion to give to a child who needs a mummy and daddy they can love and trust.

- We will bring our parenting skills of many years to nurture a child and give them security, stability and a sense of belonging.

- We will offer a loving family, home and environment essential for a child's physical, psychological, emotional and social needs and development.

- We are contributing to society by giving a child the opportunity of a better future and this child in turn having a positive effect on the wider community

- In coming forward as adoptive parents we will be an example to many other families in our community, creating more awareness and encouraging potential adoptive parents to consider adoption.

26 January 2012

Photo of one of our homework items during the preparatory course

Useful Tip

 # Keep in touch with those in your preparation course.

One of the most amazing things we did was to stay connected with the other nine people (four couples and one single mum) whom we met during our preparation course. During the adoption process, we kept in touch and met up quarterly for lunches and catch-ups. We followed each other's journeys until everyone in the group got their children. Some adopted babies, one family adopted twins, and another brought home two siblings, a boy and a girl.

Being part of this varied group also meant that we had a good mixture of ages amongst us. Meeting up from time to time has also been very beneficial for all the children, raising their confidence and making them realise that many other children are adopted, and so they are not alone. Now, our children look forward to seeing each other grow and develop. As parents, sharing our experiences, frustrations, the good and the bad, and encouraging each other has been a tremendous help. We still meet up from time to time, and in a way, we've all become one big family.

"There are times when the adoption process is exhausting and painful and makes you want to scream. But, I am told, so does childbirth."

Scott Simon

THE APPLICATION AND ASSESSMENT

Application Forms

Having taken the four-day course, we were assigned a social worker named Mr. P., who worked with us and supported us throughout the whole adoption process, right up until the time we brought our son home. Mr. P. reassured us that he was "on our side", and that we had nothing to worry about. At this stage we also filled out the official adoption application forms.

Completing the comprehensive forms was a bit daunting, almost like writing a thesis! But thankfully Mr. P. assisted us through it all. We were asked to produce a number of documents, including our personal identification documents, bank account details, utility bills and other types of records. The form also required complete addresses of every local authority where we had lived in the UK. Background checks were then carried out by the authorities in all the boroughs we named. In addition, we underwent enhanced Criminal Records Bureau (CRB) and Police National Computer (PNC) checks. We were required to supply six personal references from family and close friends, and they were each contacted individually—even those living abroad. The information they provided was confidential; therefore, none of it was disclosed to us.

Assessment

At the time we went through the process, the assessment stage was referred to as 'The Home Study.' This was the essential component of all the checks carried out to assess our suitability as adoptive parents. Our assigned social worker came to our home almost every week or two, and although the times and dates were mutually agreed upon, it still was quite challenging and time consuming. Particularly if you have work commitments, younger children at home or a very busy lifestyle, time management is of utmost importance during this phase.

At first, it felt awkward telling intimate things about ourselves to a third party, especially for me (my husband wasn't so bothered about it), but I soon got used to it. Moreover, as it was a continuous process, our assigned social worker almost became like family, as he was almost always in our home. He once even went out on his motorbike to get us milk on a day that I wasn't even aware we had run out!

Our social worker also spoke to our 12-year-old son, as well as his school, to get a picture of how our family life impacted his behaviour and studies. Mr P. also had sessions with other members of our family and friends, which included the six people we had given as references at the start of the process. The sessions took place at their homes, at various times they had agreed upon. Therefore, it's crucial to list people who know you quite well, especially because you would not know the questions those references were asked. It was a bit nerve-wracking, but the fact that our references know us quite well helped calm our anxieties.

It is absolutely crucial that prospective parents be open and honest with the social worker during the home visits. For example, we answered various questions about our past, present and future life, our weaknesses and strengths, our past partners, likes and dislikes, hobbies, extended families, religious beliefs, spending habits and finances, including our income and expenditures. Some aspects felt emotionally draining. Some of the investigative visits involved the social worker sitting with either my husband or myself separately, asking very personal questions about our individual, married and family lives. We also had sessions that involved both of us being asked questions together, as a couple, dealing with similar issues.

Overall, the assessment involved a whole lot of questioning and probing, some of which took me down memory lane of my life and my past. As a result, I had to call my mum several times to clarify some details about my childhood, things that I never knew and never bothered to ask (you just do not think that you'll need to know certain details!). I remember having to write a chronological history of myself from when I was born to date. I had to refer to a lot of old documents. Believe it or not, it was a very emotional time for me personally, because I discovered some things about my childhood that I never knew before. Issues that I thought I had overcome activated some feelings that I thought were dead and buried; instead, I found that I had to go through a new phase of healing. Yet reflecting also brought back lovely and happy memories; therefore, in the end, I'll say it all worked out as a positive experience.

Again, it is important to bear in mind that the assessment is not a ploy to catch you out, but rather a way of getting to know who you truly are. All of the information is useful when deciding on a child that you can adequately support as parents and as a family. In addition, remember that, as Mr. P. said, your social worker is 'on your side,' not against you, and that all the findings aid them in presenting an accurate record to an adoption panel. The adoption panel is not looking for 'perfect' families, as such do not exist; instead they only want to know your strengths, weaknesses, and limits, and to understand your family better. They have access to everyone and everything, and they would likely find things out even if the prospective parents were not completely honest with them. You probably would not be able to adopt if you have a criminal record for certain criminal or sexual offences. However, it is in your best interest to be honest about it all; the agency will decide if the offence should be taken into account or not. Above all, do not attempt to leave any 'skeletons in your closet.'

Useful Tips

Re-organise your life.

Currently, the adoption process is lengthy and time-consuming. Therefore, inform your family and support network beforehand that a considerable number of assessments and meetings will take up much of your time. I became self-employed before starting the process, as I was previously a civil servant who worked shifts. Though we had the assistance of an au pair, I decided to set up my own business closer to our home to give me the required flexibility. My husband worked 9 to 5 and so was only fully available at the weekends. Also, considering the age group from which we chose to adopt, we wouldn't want to leave the child, at least in the initial months, with a third party as we had with our biological son. This is not to say that everyone has to take this approach. It's just something to be aware of, so that you can plan ahead in the best way to suit your own individual family.

 # Avoid planning long holidays during the assessment period.

If you are planning a long holiday, it may be wise to take it before starting the adoption process, because long breaks during the home visits and assessments would only delay progress. However, you should be able to take short breaks or long weekend breaks without impacting the time frame. We postponed our vacations until we were through all the panel reviews and fully approved and waiting to be matched with our child. However, when the unexpected happens (such as illness and bereavement, among others), there is always room for mutual agreements and flexibility in organising and rearranging things to suit everyone's needs. Our social worker was very understanding, and he was always happy to rearrange dates or times.

"If there's a cause worth fighting for, it's this: children belong in families.

Nicole Skellenge

THE ADOPTION PANELS

We faced two separate panels in the course of our process. The panels were comprised of various professionals from the community who were independent of the local authority. They included experienced adopters, social workers and other child experts.

The first panel we faced was an approval panel, which consisted of about 12 people. When we walked into the room it was quite daunting to see all those people sitting at a long table across from us. It felt as though we were in court, about to be found guilty of an offence. We were invited to sit opposite the panel, with our social worker sitting beside us. That was a bit reassuring, as we already knew that at least he was on our side.

The duty of the panel was to make a judgement based on the information our social worker had compiled from the assessments and other information gathered about us as a couple and about our family.

Each member of the panel asked us various questions. I panicked throughout the review, yet we ensured that we responded to each question to the best of our abilities, being honest with our responses.

The second panel was the matching panel. This panel review took place after we had been through the whole adoption process and a child for whom our family was suitable had been identified. The process was similar to that of the approval panel, but the questions asked were specific to the particular child's needs. The questions included, for example, why we thought our family was suitable for him considering his circumstances and background, and what we had to offer that would be particularly beneficial to him and his future. They also asked us questions about how we would cope if he chose a different religion from ours or had a different sexual orientation.

Our experiences with both the panels seemed quite scary at the time, but in hindsight, all they were looking to achieve was to place the child in a warm and loving home, where he could grow, flourish and have a bright future, and not re-live any trauma or negative experiences he might have been through. I can assure you that there is absolutely nothing to be terrified of and that your social worker probably would warn you in advance if they envisaged any major issues or problems. It's quite reassuring that the whole process is thorough, and every aspect is considered very well, as it protects you, the adoptive parents, as well as the child.

THE MATCHING PROCESS

During the matching process the family, who has been approved by the approval panel, is matched with a child. In the matching process, the search is for a suitable family as is in the best interest of the child. It is the family who would have to convince the authorities that their home is suitable. Up until this time we did not know what child we would be adopting. We had indicated the age range we would prefer, but we were open about the gender. We were both working parents, and we had a 12-year-old son in school, so we were honest and realistic with what we were able to cope with at the time

You may also want to indicate your capacity to raise a child with learning difficulties, considering your current family situation. We knew we would not be able to cope with a child with severe physical disabilities, for example, especially if they needed full-time care. We were happy to adopt a child with mild disabilities or learning difficulties, however. It is very important to examine yourselves and your family situation and then make an informed and accurate assessment before making a decision.

We discovered that our son had been in care well before we came forward to be considered as adoptive parents. However, the way the system worked was that prospective adoptive parents would have to successfully complete the approval process before being considered for any child who is ready to be adopted. Then, when we saw the photograph of our son, he melted our hearts immediately. We discussed it as a family, and all agreed there was no turning back—he was the one!

By the time we went through the whole process, our son was just a month away from his fourth birthday. He was already viewed as a child who might end up in long-term care. As a black boy who was almost four years old, we discovered, it was less likely for families to come forward to adopt him. In part, this is because of a negative stereotype surrounding older boys, especially boys from ethnic minority backgrounds. And so ours was the first family to consider adopting him. Otherwise, he probably would have stayed in long-term fostering until he turned 18, leaving the Care system as an adult to figure life out alone, with very little support and no real family. So, it seemed we got there just at the right time to bring him home to become part of our family.

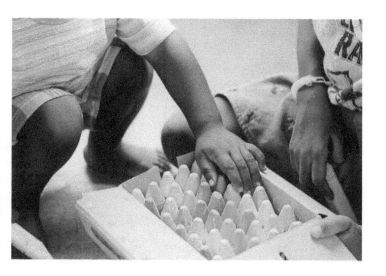

> Adoption is not about finding children for families, it is about finding families for children.

Joyce Maguire Pavao

MEETING OUR SON

The introduction and transition were supposed to occur in a two-week window, although it may take longer if the process does not go as planned. Also, it could be stopped altogether, if something goes wrong or the process breaks down for any reason.

Our son had lived with a foster family since the time he was taken into care. As we had been identified as adoptive parents for him, his social worker and his foster mother had started preparing him for the transition by telling him stories about 'forever families' through various books and videos. He partially understood that the work of his social worker, whom he saw as a friend, was to find families for children who didn't have them.

On our side, his room was ready, completely decorated with 'Thomas the Tank Engine' paraphernalia. We were told that was his favourite character, and so his bedding, curtains, clock, and lampshade were all decorated with images of

Thomas. We were also asked to produce a video recording introducing ourselves and showing his room and all other parts of our home. Finally, we put together an album of pictures of ourselves and our home. All these were sent to our son ahead of our initial visit.

Our son's room was 'Thomas the Tank Engine' themed.

It was a very sensitive period for everyone involved, even more so for our son, who was less than four years old at the time. He had been in care for more than three years. We started off with a visit to meet our son in person at his foster mother's home. It was only my husband and myself; we did not take any other family member at this stage. Although it was a casual visit, he already knew we were coming to meet him for the first time. (After he was settled in our home, he told us that he had known a lot of people had 'meetings' about him, and that he always wondered if he was being taken somewhere else.)

The visit was in the company of our son's social worker and his foster mother. We were introduced by our names, and our son immediately engaged in conversation with us. He asked a few cheeky questions, and we felt a connection instantly. We sat down in the living room, and he showed us some of his toys and books. He was clearly excited but cautious. He kept looking back at his foster mum for reassurance, which made him feel safe. The visit lasted about 40 minutes, and then we went home.

A couple of days later we returned to the foster mum's home, but this time, we went out from the house to a café for coffee, both of us, our son and his foster mother. It was all about getting familiar and gaining his trust. We sat for about an hour and chatted quite a lot. We went back a few times, sometimes to help with his evening bath and bedtime, and at other times we went to help him at breakfast. His foster mum eventually brought him to our home for a visit. Then we progressed to taking him out by ourselves to the shops for a day, or bringing him from his foster mum's home to ours for a day. Finally, he spent a night at home with us, and he never went back. It was decided that because the transition went a lot better than expected, there was no reason to extend it. So, our son came home to stay with us, and it all happened a few days short of the planned two-week window.

The whole process went smoothly, in part because our son liked our home, especially his room, and because he enjoyed playing with his brother, our biological son, who was twelve years old at the time. Because we had a lot of information about the things our adopted son loved most, we were able to prepare our home and his surroundings to his liking. We were patient, loving and attentive towards him. Whenever he was with us, he was included in some of the discussions, such as what to have for lunch or dinner, or what to watch on television. As a result, during the times he visited, he fell in love with our home and our family, and he really wanted to be part of our household.

Useful Tip

 # Get a lot of training and practice with children.

It is advisable that you get adequate training and practice with children, particularly if you have no children or have not been around children very much. If you have young nieces, nephews, godchildren or others, try to get more involved with them; offer to take them home for weekends or take them out to the cinema, theatres, restaurants, and playgroups, among other options. You might also volunteer at nurseries, after-school clubs, summer camps and such places. The more time you spend with children, the more experience you will get. Read books, magazines, blogs, and articles about children and child development as well. Speaking to parents and asking as many questions as possible will help you to equip yourself. Remember: seeing or knowing children from afar is not the same as actually having to live with and care for them.

Also, consider the fact that your adopted child may be an only child if you do not have other child in your home. An only child can get lonely after the toddler age and children always crave to play with their own age mates. Having a network of other nearby parents and children would be useful when they reach the stage of needing the company of their age group.

THE TEN-WEEK WAIT

We brought our adopted son home in January 2013, but we were only half-way through the journey. A mandatory waiting period of ten weeks followed, from the time we brought our son home to live with us to the time we could put in an application to the courts to legally adopt him. During that period, our son's social worker made regular visits to our home to assess how he was settling in with us as a family, as well as how he was progressing in all aspects of his development. The social worker would also make necessary recommendations and help with whatever issues arose. In addition, we had the support of our own social worker, Mr. P.

However, we didn't realise that this waiting period was the time to ensure we exhausted all the necessary help or support we could get. Our son was still considered a 'looked-after child' at that point. Once the adoption became official, we didn't receive the level of support we expected with certain issues we faced.

The ten-week wait is also the time to integrate your child into your family, teaching them your values and standards, amongst other things. It is important to start raising the child as your own and not to treat them like a guest, or in a way you think would cause the child to accept you. If the rules and boundaries are not put in place from the start, it can be very be difficult to try changing routines later.

This time too was a very sensitive period for us as a family, because we had to take some time off at home for him to settle in. Why did we do so? Because our son was almost four years old when we took him in, he could remember things about his foster mother, and so he refused to call me mum for a while. In addition, he had behavioural issues. He would wet himself sometimes, and on one or two occasions, he even defecated in his pants. He would slam doors, scream and occasionally destroy things.

Prior to the transition stage, his social worker had informed us that we would need to be firm and ensure that we set strict boundaries, because it had been lacking in his upbringing. He had been allowed to have his way in a majority of instances, with unnecessary indulgences. Because his foster mother was an older lady, we believe that she might have been more lenient, and that he might have lacked discipline in his day-to-day life. We were fully aware of all these issues, and we were mentally prepared to deal with those challenges. It was quite tough, but we were resilient; we focused on the end result and the reason we started out in the first place.

Due to all of these issues, our son could not initially attend a nursery. Instead, I took him to playgroups, libraries and children centres, but I had to stay close to him and keep a close watch on his interaction with other children. We realised that he loved creating things from paper, cardboard, colour-pencils and crayons, so we got him lots of supplies to get him busy.

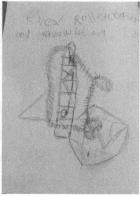

He enjoyed colouring and creativity.

Through all these challenges, we learned to love, to care and to set boundaries, where necessary, for our child. We were determined to make it work, and gradually we made it clear to him through our actions that we were not going to give up on him. After the ten-week waiting period, we filled out the necessary forms and applied to the courts, and we were given a date for the ceremony.

All the hard work, patience and persistence paid off. Our son gradually started to get better in his behaviour, and I got used to the task at hand. It all became easier, because we had developed a routine and rules, and he eventually started to call us mum and dad. His highlight was his older brother, whom he loved, and he enjoyed their periods of creativity and rough play on our sitting room rug. They both had a whole load of fun and good times! That rug became their favourite play area, and our son adored the fact that he was part of a family. Whenever either my husband or myself were going out, he would ask when we would be back, and he would tell us that he liked it better when we were all at home together as a family. Also, whenever we took him out, or whenever he had the opportunity, the first thing he would tell anyone in conversation was that he has a big brother and his brother's name. He would also tell anyone who had time to listen all the fun he had with his brother on their favourite play rug.

We were bonding as a family and everything was fitting together in our home. We were dealing with whatever challenge came up. We had come a long way, and we knew that there wasn't anything we couldn't eventually navigate through.

The favourite play rug

Useful Tips

 # Identify your support network beforehand.

You will need your friends and family along with you as you proceed in the adoption process. Although you may not want to involve a whole bunch of people initially, you would need a handful of people you trust to be there for you when needed. Their assistance could be of great value when you just feel overwhelmed and want someone to talk to or need some sort of support in caring for your child. They may include friends, neighbours, and people you can rely on or are comfortable with.

For example, when we took our son home, we were advised to avoid introducing him to anyone other than the three immediate family members (my husband and I, plus our biological son). This was quite difficult as I decided to stay at home with him for four months to get him settled properly, due to his circumstances at the time we adopted him. We were also advised that it was in his best interests not to attend school for a while, as he was only four years old at the time. Going to school immediately might get him confused, as it would mean too many new people to get used to all at once, and that could be a detriment to him settling in at home.

During that period, I needed a lot of support, because I spent the days alone at home with him while my husband was at work and our older son at school. It was quite overwhelming to manage a child—who had a few behavioural issues and no boundaries—all by myself from Monday to Friday for four months! It was very helpful that I was able to speak to friends and family members, one of whom was a foster carer. Sometimes it was just having them listen to all the challenges I was facing that made the difference, getting things off my chest was useful.

Also, you may need someone who can relieve you for a couple of hours when you need to take a break. So, after the initial four months of family bonding, we introduced him to a family friend. She would visit us once in a while, and our son liked her, which really helped. Sometimes she would come to the house, and we would sit and watch TV, have tea and chat together. She would also get down on the carpet and play with our son. Although I was always there with them, it made a lot of difference to me emotionally and mentally that she was present.

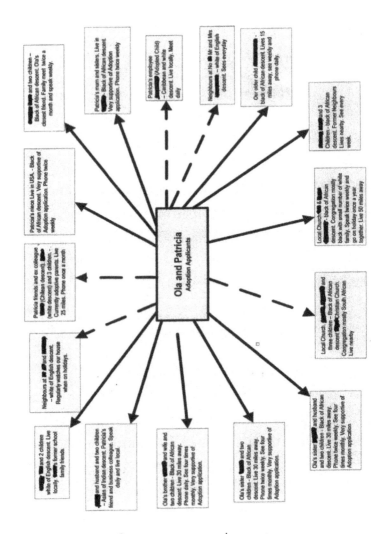

Our support network exercise

 # Do not be scared to accept the 'SEN Label' for your child.

"SEN" stood for "Statement of Special Educational Needs." However, since the introduction of the Children and Families Act 2014, it has been replaced by Education Health and Care Plans (EHCP). This plan is a legally binding document, which sets out a child or young person's special educational needs.

When we got our son, we were warned that he was not used to having any boundaries set for him, and we clearly saw that he had huge behavioural problems. However, to be honest, we were in denial, and as Christians, we believed that we would get through things with prayer. We discovered only later that applying for an SEN would have better protected our son and allowed him to benefit from extra support that the school does not usually provide. Such support is only available through the extra funding provided by the local authority and it secures the best possible outcomes for a child in education, health and social care. However, at the time, we had thought that it was a negative label, which we did not want for our child, and so we refused even to consider it.

After staying at home with our son for four months, we enrolled him at a local primary school. He didn't settle in quickly, however, because he was in a class of about 60 children. It was overwhelming for him, because he had always had full attention. Also, the head teacher at the school was not supportive, and it seemed that she was not happy to have our son in her school. Our son continued to have many issues. He would wet himself daily at school. Other incidents included claims of him pulling a teacher's lanyard from their neck, emptying another child's water bottle or playing with another child's hair from behind. We got called in almost every day for one incident or another. There were also instances of teachers reporting that our son would crawl across the carpet to distract others during the 15-minute structured learning period.

We expected the school to at least understand that our son had recently been brought into our home and was in the process of settling down. Also, the school did not consider the fact that he was a four-year-old child in a completely new environment having to cope in a class of 59 other reception children. The school only complained that it was negative attention seeking, and that they could not cope with it.

We had a few meetings with the teachers, the Special Educational Needs Coordinator (SENCO) and the Local Authority's Educational Representative to discuss ways of working together. It was also decided that the school should invite the assistance of an Educational Psychologist (EP) to work with our son. However, the head teacher still managed to exclude our son less than a year of him enrolling at the school, without exhausting all the options agreed upon at our various meetings. This would not have been possible if we had an SEN in place for him at the time, as statemented children could not be excluded. Instead, he would have been protected, and he would have had access to extra support by way of funding from the local authority.

These issues were learning curves for us, and we worked through all the obstacles with determination and resilience. We discovered that we had to be firm, assertive and stand up to the school for the sake of our son. We wrote letters to the school governors and to our local MP for assistance. Eventually we were able to get our son into a different school, where he settled and thrived. With time, all the pain of the ordeal with the former school healed and fizzled away, and our son successfully completed Year Six at the new school.

THE FORMAL ADOPTION CEREMONY

Finally, the ten-week period came to an end, and the day of the formal adoption procedure arrived. It was all very exciting! The ceremony took place at a designated Magistrate Court within our county. It involved our son, my husband and I, both our social workers, some court officials and the Judge. A little ceremony was held, there was the reading out of some details, and the Judge asked our son some questions. Although it was meant to be a formal process, it wasn't carried out in a way that made our son uncomfortable. It was conducted in a way that made the process feel like fun to him. A few pictures were taken, with lots of smiles words of encouragement from everyone around, which made our son feel at ease. We saw our son beaming with excitement, as it was a very important day for him.

Our son was awarded an Adoption Certificate with his new name and family name. He was also given a little teddy bear. We took a few group photographs with everyone in the room including the Judge. The event helped to increase our son's confidence, as it was an assurance that he was here to stay, truly a part of the family. The certificate has always been in his room, at his request, and he treasures it very much.

Although the event is largely ceremonial, the authority of the court seals the process. It makes your adopted child legally your own, taking on your name, with no legal ties whatsoever with the child's biological parents. In order words, the child's biological parents cannot lay claim on the child. When the child turns 18, adopted children may decide to find their biological parents; but whatever happens in future, the tie with the adoptive family can never be severed or forgotten.

We have a twice-a-year 'Letter Box Contact' with our son's biological mother. The way it works is that we write twice a year, sharing our son's progress, his likes, dislikes, etc., and she replies to our letter. All correspondence goes via the local authority's Children's Services. We write and send our letters to them, they read the contents and only send it off if they are satisfied with the contents. The same happens from her side before they send her letter to us. There are very strict guidelines for the wordings of the letters. They cannot contain words or phrases that would stimulate or cause unnecessary emotional upset for the child. If the local authority staff are not satisfied with the contents or certain phrases, they'll return the letter to the writer to amend or rewrite it before onward transmission to the party concerned.

Various levels of contact are usually arranged for the child and the biological parents if they are still alive and reachable. Some have no contact at all, and some have periodic, supervised face-to-face contact at designated places. It all depends on various factors beyond the scope of this book. The most important fact is that the Adoption Ceremony seals the process, you are fully responsible for your child.

Useful Tips

*# Get things done while your child is still a
'looked-after child.'*

When you finally take your child home, it will take
another ten weeks before you can apply to the courts
to officially adopt your child. During this period,
up until the courts approve your application, your
child is a 'looked-after child' by the authorities.
This status gives your child preference or priority in
certain circumstances. For instance, when applying
to schools or nurseries, they get priority on the list.
Otherwise, you would have to push to get certain
things done during this period.

In our case, we were advised not to send our
son to school immediately (as I explained earlier).
Therefore, we missed out on the school we wanted,
because the school had a preference for children
who had an SEN and for looked-after children. Our
social worker was not in a hurry to apply to the
school, and we couldn't do it by ourselves, because
we didn't physically have our son at home with us at
the time and we were busy going through the process
of bringing him home. If we had been aware of the

importance of securing a place for him at that time, we would have been prompt and ensured that the authorities secured the school within the required time frame.

Also, we did not get much help from the local authority on various matters once the courts had approved our application to adopt, with our son's status which had changed from 'looked-after' to 'adopted'. This included the issues we faced when he eventually started school, help with child specialists for his behavioural issues at the time and many other matters that we had to sort out ourselves, all of which would have been a lot easier if the local authority had dealt with them.

However, the law has changed now, and adopted children are now seen as previously looked-after children and can enjoy all the privileges they had before adoption. I believe it's still a lot easier to get issues resolved by the adoption agency or local authority before you bring your child home to live with you. Issues would get resolved more quickly before the child crosses over to your home, at least the matters that can be dealt with prior. We found that once our son was at home with us, we had to be much more proactive in getting things moving. We believe that this is because once a child has been placed safely with a family, the focus shifts to the many other children who need families, and they become the priority.

 # Research thoroughly the options for financial assistance.

We did not receive ongoing financial support from our local authority. We were asked to keep the receipts for reimbursement for some new items we bought solely in preparation for bringing our son home. We were able to keep the receipts for a new bed, mattress, wallpaper and curtains, among others. It all came to about £500. The local authority did pay it back, but it took a while. We later discovered that some families got ongoing financial support on top of the initial expenditure, and that some local authorities or private adoption agencies offer financial support either as a lump sum or on a regular basis. So ensure that you make enquiries from the onset about your options for financial assistance. Remember: caring for a child is a huge financial commitment and takes a massive toll on your finances.

I suppose we didn't get it because we didn't ask, and we didn't ask because we weren't expecting it, as we were not aware that such funds were available to adoptive parents. We assumed that only foster families are entitled to financial support. Even if you are not entitled to general financial assistance, there may be other types of funds you can access, for instance, if your child has an ongoing medical condition or needs regular hospital visits. You would need to research or ask for these funds, because most of the time you would not be informed.

POST ADOPTION SUPPORT

Both the adoptive parents and the adopted child might need some level of ongoing support even after the child has settled in with their adoptive family. Adopted children identify with their adopted family but also have their own identity as an adopted child. Some children may start to ask questions to understand what has happened to their biological parents or become curious about their origins. It is crucial to be open and honest with your adopted child, especially those children who were too young at time of adoption to realise that they are not being raised by their biological parents. This would prevent the child trying to snoop around trying to find information secretly or turning to the wrong source in search of details about their past.

A good way to initiate such conversations is through the child's 'Life Story Book' It is a book that is handed to adoptive parents with their adopted child, containing information about what has happened to the child in life. These books are similar to scrapbooks or photo albums, they usually have some details about the birth family, previous placements, the child's baby pictures, why they were adopted and many other details and photos which would help the child understand their history and background. It is essential to share the contents with your child, but it has to be at the right time. You may decide to take your child through various aspects of the book depending on the questions they ask. It is entirely up to you how and when you do it, you would get to know your child and you can determine the appropriate pace.

We found that taking our son through his Life Story Book allowed him to open up more about his feelings and it triggered a few more questions and comments from him. It made him more comfortable to talk about what he remembered of his past placements and the people he met. He was able to speak freely about what he enjoyed most at his previous foster family and incidents he did not like about some of the periods he went into respite with another family. We noticed that it helped his self-esteem as he became more confident in many aspects, he would put himself forward more to participate in more activities, at school, parties and other family gatherings. The more we spoke about the contents of the book the more he developed a better sense of security and permanence. It all reflected in a change in the type of questions he asked and his spontaneous comments.

There are usually various training workshops, social events and various other support networks that would be recommended through the Adoption Agency or Local Authority that placed your child. Your social worker should be there to link you with other professional assistance if they are unable to give you adequate support. It is important to access these avenues and attend as many events as you can. Some are just for adoptive parents but some are also beneficial for children. You may be able to get specialised one-to-one support or counselling to help in dealing with more complicated issues. Some agencies also have a pool of other adoptive parents who are happy to support new adoptive families by answering questions and helping them through difficult situations, drawing on their own experiences. There are various agencies and organisations out there willing to help you get through various ongoing issues.

"My birth mother brought me into this world, but it was my adoptive parents who gave me life."

Christiana Romo

CONCLUSION

Opinions differ about adopting children; some are negative, probably based on some adoptive families' difficult experiences or a negative stereotype that is often associated with adoption. However, there are numerous success stories of children who were adopted and went on to became great men and women in society. Jamie Foxx, the American actor, was adopted shortly after his birth. He has often acknowledged his adoptive family's influence in his life as one of the greatest reasons for his success. The late Steve Jobs, CEO and co-founder of Apple Inc., was also an adopted child. His adoptive parents had said that Steve was a very difficult child, and they considered returning him when he was two years old. However, they endured the difficulty and raised someone who became a huge blessing to the world. Steve Jobs himself later said he felt he had been "really blessed by having the two of them as parents." There are so many other positive stories of adopted children and families. It is therefore important to focus on the positive aspects and outcome of adoption.

Adoption is a lifelong commitment. We see our adopted child as our own, and we are growing together as a family daily, as well as ensuring that he is being included and accepted by our extended family and friends. We are also learning and discovering new things and ways to achieve the best for him on a daily basis. Even though we have raised our own biological children, it is important to be mindful of the fact that all children are different. Depending on your adopted child's previous experiences, insecurities, traumas or fears, you would surely have to raise him or her differently, focusing on the best interest of the child.

There is not a 'one-size-fits-all' approach to adoption as every adoption journey is unique. We are learning and discovering the best ways to deal with situations every day as issues arise. Our son knew from the onset that he has living biological parents, and we get asked different questions at different stages of his development and maturity. We always endeavour to give responses that are as honest as possible. We as parents have studied and known our son to a certain extent, and we are therefore able to decide how much to tell him at any particular stage, or, better still, how we should respond to his questions, considering the fact that he is sensitive and at the same time curious. We have to weigh the options of telling him the full truth at a specific time against hurting his feelings. We are always assessing all our discussions and responses to ensure they are age-appropriate and to decide whether he can emotionally handle the information at that particular time.

We sometimes avoid discussing sensitive topics when our son is present, especially things that we have no information about whatsoever. For instance, specific details about his birth or his biological family history are issues we would not bring up unless he asks about them. Our aim is to continue to handle all matters to the best of our ability and in the best interests of our son and our family as a whole.

There exists a world of information and references to draw upon. Policies are changing, and various organisations are constantly innovating and working towards making the whole journey and process easier while supporting adoptive families. Our adoption journey is ongoing, and it's well worth it. Seeing your child daily, the transformation and the difference you are making in their life, is extremely rewarding.

"Adoption isn't just a childhood experience; it is a life-long experience.

DaSanne Stokes

REFERENCES

- **adoption.com**

- **Adoption.Net**

- **www.adoptionuk.org** Adoption Facts and Figures for England

- **www.bbc.co.uk** BBC, Schools Parents, What is a Statement of Special Needs?

- Preparing to Adopt: A Training Pack for Preparation Groups by Eileen Fursland

- The Bible: New Living Translation (NLT)

- **www.dictionary.com**

- **www.familylives.org.uk** Adopting a Child

- **www.first4adoption.org.uk** 10 Common Misconceptions Quashed

- **www.gov.uk** National Statistics, Children Looked After in England Including Adoption: 2016 to 2017

- **www.hounslowadoption.org.uk** Adoption: A Step-by-Step Guide

- **www.ipsea.org.uk**

- **www.nspcc.org.uk** Children in Care: Our Work with Looked-After Children, the Challenges in Care, and What the Law Says

- **www.theguardian.com** Adoption Numbers Drop Steeply as Government's Flagship Policy Falters (by Patrick Butler, 29 September 2016)

Useful Websites and Organisations

- **www.adoptionuk**

- **www.corambaaf.org.uk**

- **www.gov.uk**

Further Reading

- *Adopting a Child: A Guide for People Interested in Adoption* by Jenifer Lord

- *Parenting Your Adopted Child* by Andrew Adesman

- *The Adopter's Handbook: Information, Resources and Services for Adoptive Parents* by BAAF

ABOUT THE AUTHOR

Patricia Dopemu is a mother and grandmother … committed to helping children and creating strong families through adoption.

She has a law degree, LLB (HONS) and worked in family law—supporting families going through various difficult life changes. She also spent many years at the UK Border Force, where she was part of the Children and Young Person's Team—aimed to protect unaccompanied minors and children involved in abductions or human trafficking.

Patricia is the founder of Passion for the Unreached Foundation—a charity to help the less fortunate. She also operates a website she created to encourage prospective adoptive parents … and serve as a platform to support adoptive families: youtoocanadopt.com.

Patricia lives in London with her husband. They are blessed with three children and three grandchildren. On the weekend, you will find her singing Gospel music at church … and cooking up her famous Jollof rice for her family.

Contact the author at
www.youtoocanadopt.com

Black children in London are waiting longer to be adopted and we need more families to adopt them.

Like Patricia, families are opening their hearts, sharing their traditions and teaching their adopted children about their culture, helping them to thrive.

Adopt London finds adoptive families for children from African, Caribbean, Asian and mixed ethnic backgrounds. We support single people and couples from all communities throughout their adoption journey to create new forever families for London children.

We also welcome families who would like to adopt a child of a different ethnicity, religion and culture from their own. We encourage all our families to embrace and celebrate their adopted child's identity.

If you are interested in knowing more about Adopt London, to change a child's life and your own, please visit our website

www.adoptlondon.org.uk

At Alpha Childcare we offer high quality, affordable, childcare and education for all children from 3 months to 11 years. We have nurseries, preschool and out of school clubs in Eltham, Greenwich, Hackney, Rainham and Canning Town.

Carefully designed setting to be homely, inviting, safe, and secure.

We encourage children to learn independently in a fun, healthy and nurturing environment.

Our menus are carefully designed to offer a healthy, balanced diet.

We welcome all children and families in an inclusive environment.

Alpha Childcare Franchise Opportunity

"Let's make it happen!"

We are excited to offer you the opportunity to become an Alpha Franchisee.
For more information, please contact us on
020 8469 1888.

020 8469 1888
info@alphachildcare.com
www.alphachildcare.com